'CHRIST-CEN

AN1

'FAITH WITH FOCUS - ONE THING'

BRIAN JOHNSTON

Published by:

HAYES PRESS Publisher, Resources & Media,

The Barn, Flaxlands

Royal Wootton Bassett

Swindon, SN4 8DY

United Kingdom

www.hayespress.org

The author wishes to acknowledge that the chapter headings used in this book broadly follow those used by John Stott in his book "Focus on Christ", which was published by Kingsway Publications in 1979.

CHAPTER ONE: THROUGH CHRIST (OUR MEDIATOR)

The idea of having to go through official channels seems to give us the impression of remoteness - as when we demand to see the manager! We get frustrated when we can't go directly to the person in charge. But nothing could be further from the truth when, in the Bible, we read about going through Jesus Christ to God. The remoteness was our own doing: the gulf between God and man was caused by human disobedience. It's in Jesus Christ that God becomes accessible to us - it's in Jesus Christ that God makes himself available to us. Our access to God is through Jesus Christ, his Son. As we read the early verses of Romans chapter 5, look out for the number of times the word 'through' (Greek: 'dia') is used:

> "Therefore, having been justified by faith, we have peace with God through our Lord Jesus Christ, through whom also we have obtained our introduction by faith into this grace in which we stand ... But God demonstrates His own love toward us, in that while we were yet sinners, Christ died for us. Much more then, having now been justified by His blood, we shall be saved from the wrath of God through Him. For if while we were enemies we were reconciled to God through the death of His Son, much more, having been reconciled, we shall be saved by His life. And not only this, but we also exult in God through our Lord Jesus Christ, through whom we have now received the reconciliation" (Romans 5:1-11 NASB).

The word 'through' occurs 6 times in that reading from Romans 5, a section which emphasizes that our access to God is based on the perfect life of Jesus Christ surrendered to God on the cross, and beyond that, it's also based on Jesus' life now. For it tells us that the preservation of our earthly lives in service for the Lord is based upon his heavenly resurrection life of service as he appears in the presence of God for us. Our souls are saved by his death, and our lives of service are saved by his life above.

The two ideas presented there in Romans chapter 5: those of Jesus coming out from God to reveal God to us by his going to the cross, and of his returning to heaven to appear before God for us there, draw our attention to the two aspects of his work as the mediator between God and us. It's a work that's uniquely his, for the apostle Paul wrote in his first letter to Timothy: "For there is one God, and one mediator also between God and men, the man Christ Jesus, who gave Himself as a ransom for all, the testimony given at the proper time" (1 Timothy 2:5,6).

This work of being a mediator is like a two-way street. Let's try to explain more about its two aspects by thinking of the actions of speaking and representing. God has spoken to us finally through Jesus Christ, and we speak to God through Jesus Christ. He's the one and only mediator, and both the role of apostle and high priest are his. Jesus Christ came from heaven to earth as the great apostle so that he might represent God to us; and he returned to heaven after his death and resurrection so that he might represent us to God.

In the Old Testament, there was a school of prophets and a family of priests. Through the succession of the prophets God communicated his message to his people; and by means of the system of priests the people were able to draw near to God. The word for 'priest' in the Bible seems to come from the idea of 'mediating in religious services'. The priest was the people's representative before God, just as the prophet was God's representative to them. Now the Jews would usually regard Moses as the greatest of the prophets; and perhaps they would look to Aaron as being the greatest of the priests – certainly he was the first in the line of priests established at the time of his brother Moses – but the New Testament letter written to the Hebrews was written to Jewish converts to assure them that Jesus was far greater than both Moses and Aaron! Both offices – that of prophet and that of priest – were combined in Jesus. Let's remind ourselves as to how that letter begins:

> "God, after He spoke long ago to the fathers in the prophets in many portions and in many ways, in these last days has spoken to us in His Son, whom He appointed heir of all things, through whom also He made the world. And He is the radiance of His glory and the exact representation of His nature, and upholds all things by the word of His power. When He had made purification of sins, He sat down at the right hand of the Majesty on high, having become as much better than the angels, as He has inherited a more excellent name than they" (Hebrews 1:1-4).

This is one of the Bible's most wonderful descriptions of the Lord Jesus in all his divine majesty. Later in the same letter (Hebrews 12:24; see also Hebrews 7:22), he's referred to as a mediator: the mediator of a better covenant, it says – better than the one Moses mediated (Galatians 3:19). The law came through Moses, but grace and truth came through Jesus Christ (John 1:17). And yet, even here in those tremendous opening words of Hebrews chapter 1 which we've read, we can already trace the theme of Christ as mediator – of how, while on earth, he was God's spokesperson to us; and how, now that he's back in heaven, he's our spokesperson to God.

Yes, God has spoken to us in His Son, we're told in Hebrews chapter 1. Many Bible translations give the wording as God speaking in His Son to us; but others translate it as God speaking to us 'through' or at least by Jesus Christ – which very much relates to the thought of Christ as our mediator. The prophets were merely agents of God's communication, his revelation - human instruments which God used. But it's altogether different when it comes to God's Son, Jesus. It's God himself, as Son, who's speaking. For we're told that Jesus is the 'express image' of the Father.

The word 'image' was quite a colourful one: in those New Testament days, it was used to describe the impression that a die or stamp might make in soft wax or on a coin. The idea was of two things being individually or personally distinct but yet completely equivalent, just as the Father and His Son. We still sometimes use a hand stamp. Once it's inked, it can be used to print an address on a leaflet for distribution. Anyone who's ever done this quickly realizes that any mark on the stamp is faithfully reproduced on the paper. That's the idea here. There's nothing in the Father that's not in the Son - and vice versa, speaking of their essential nature or character. What this is proclaiming is the clear message that God's Son, Jesus, bears all the characteristic marks of deity.

Not only does He bear all the distinguishing features of deity, but He bears, or upholds 'all things by the word of his power'. When Moses, back in the book of Numbers chapter 11, complained to God that he couldn't bear all the people alone, it was the equivalent word to the one used of Jesus Christ. Definitely, a greater than Moses is here! But He who bears all the distinguishing marks of deity; He who bears all things on his almighty shoulders, once bore our sins in his body on the tree of Calvary! For we read "he ... by himself, purged our sins". Amazing grace!

Finally, in this introduction, we're told He's now seated in heaven. Four times, in fact, the letter to the Hebrews emphasizes He's seated with God on high (Hebrews 1:3; 8:1; 10:12; 12:2) – in heaven where He's now become the High Priest on behalf of all God's people. That returns us to the matter we've been tracing: that of Jesus as the mediator between us and God. "He ... made purification of sins" (see Hebrews 10:11,12). Now as priest in heaven, Jesus applies the value of His own sacrifice on earth in bringing us to God, for example as a worshiping people.

So, indeed, Jesus the mediator, through whom God has spoken in these last days, is a greater prophet than Moses; and, now in resurrection, as seated with God on high with all His sacrificial work on earth completed, He's a greater priest than Aaron. He came out to lead us in - what a mediator! God has spoken to us through Him; and now the people of God speak to God through Him as our great high priest. Praise the Lord that both our acceptance and our access is through Christ!

CHAPTER TWO: ON CHRIST (OUR FOUNDATION)

A missionary working among hostile tribes was struggling to translate the word 'to believe' or 'to trust'. The tribes-people were cannibals and they didn't trust anyone, so how could the missionary find any expression they'd understand in order to serve his purpose? One day his servant came into his study while he was still seated at his desk. The missionary sat back in his chair and lifted his feet off the floor. 'What am I doing?' he asked the servant. The man replied using a word in their language which meant 'to lean your whole weight upon'. That's how the missionary found the right word to use. He was really trusting the chair when he lent his whole weight on it.

In fact, to illustrate the idea that trusting is the thought of 'relying on', as in the case of our leaning our full weight on something, we could have taken a Bible example from the time when the Assyrians were besieging King Hezekiah at Jerusalem. For we read in the Second book of Kings, chapter 18:

> "Then [the spokesperson for the attackers] said to them, "Say now to Hezekiah, 'Thus says the great king, the king of Assyria, "What is this confidence that you have? "You say (but they are only empty words), 'I have counsel and strength for the war.' Now on whom do you rely, that you have rebelled against me? "Now behold, you rely on the staff of this crushed reed, even on Egypt; on which if a man leans, it will go into his hand and pierce it. So is Pharaoh king of Egypt to all

who rely on him" (2 Kings 18:19-21; see also Isaiah 36:4-6).

It's clear there, too, that trusting on someone means relying on someone, and is pictured by leaning on a staff. Several times the New Testament of the Bible literally has the wording 'to believe **on**' (on not in, that is, 'epi' not 'eis'; e.g. Acts 16:31; cf. 9:42; 11:17; 22:19) in the emphatic sense of 'to rely entirely on with full assurance'.

But as well as believing on Jesus Christ, the Son of God, we're commanded to build on Him, that is to build our lives on Him. Believing on Him brings the eternal blessing of forgiveness. To believe on Jesus Christ as our saviour means we can rely entirely on Him with full assurance for salvation from the judgement of God, a salvation which we can never lose. But having trusted Him for the salvation of our souls, we should entrust Him with our day to day lives, by building our lives on Him - on what He has taught us. In Matthew's Gospel chapter 7:24-27 Jesus says:

> "... everyone who hears these words of Mine and acts on them, may be compared to a wise man who built his house on the rock. And the rain fell, and the floods came, and the winds blew and slammed against that house; and yet it did not fall, for it had been founded on the rock. Everyone who hears these words of Mine and does not act on them, will be like a foolish man who built his house on the sand. The rain fell, and the floods came, and the winds blew and slammed against that house; and it fell - and great was its fall."

You can check out whether you're wise or foolish by asking yourself if you've put Jesus' words into practice in your life. It's so important to have a good foundation. No building is better than its foundation. Having a good foundation is the secret. Just ask people who've survived living in an earthquake zone. People who live in earthquake zones surely know the value of building on solid bed-rock. The hazards for buildings on soft soil in areas liable to earthquakes are so much greater. Soft soil can settle after being compacted by the shock-waves of the 'quake; and the vibrations can cause a rise of the water-table which turns the ground into something like soup – hardly a stable foundation!

The Lord Jesus intends that our lives should be 'founded on the rock' – that we should be 'rock-solid' in the storms of life. Getting a solid basis for life – and eternity - begins when we trust in Jesus, God's Son, for salvation as the famous conversation between Jesus and his disciple Peter shows:

> "Now when Jesus came into the district of Caesarea Philippi, He was asking His disciples, "Who do people say that the Son of Man is?" And they said, "Some say John the Baptist; and others, Elijah; but still others, Jeremiah, or one of the prophets." He said to them, "But who do you say that I am?" Simon Peter answered, "You are the Christ, the Son of the living God." And Jesus said to him, "Blessed are you, Simon Barjona, because flesh and blood did not reveal this to you, but My Father who is in heaven. I also say to you that you are Peter, and upon this rock I will build My church; and the gates of Hades will not overpower it" (Matthew 16:14-18).

No doubt you're aware that there's been great controversy over the meaning of the words 'upon this rock I will build My church'. If we were to follow the majority of early interpreters, we'd be bound to say that the 'rock' was more likely to be 'the faith professed by Peter, not Peter professing the faith'. Peter, as the historical record of the Book of Acts shows, was the one who first opened the door of faith to both Jew (Acts 2) and Gentile (Acts 10). Such saving faith - of which Peter and others were merely the preachers – was always clearly proclaimed as being based totally and exclusively on Christ himself. Associated with this Church - and the profession of faith by which means we enter into membership of it - we have the picture of a 'rock'.

But Peter himself, writing later in the Bible, employs different imagery. He quotes no less than 3 different Old Testament texts about stones, and applies them all to Christ. He (in 1 Peter 2:4-8) makes clear that Jesus is the "cornerstone that's chosen and precious" of Isaiah chapter 28, as well as being 'the head of the corner' of Psalm 118, and the "stone that will make men stumble" of Isaiah 8. Why the change of imagery from rock to stone(s)? If we read Peter's letter carefully, we discover his application is to something beyond salvation. For he's not only writing to persons who had a saving faith in Jesus Christ (1 Peter 1:23), but to persons who'd also been baptized (1 Peter 3:21), and were being obedient in their faithful service for the Lord throughout the New Testament churches (1 Peter 1:1,2).

The difference between rock and stone is significant in these references as compared with the Lord's words in Matthew's Gospel. The immovable, rock-like truth of the Gospel is the basis of our secure salvation through faith alone; but Peter's references to a stone and stones, together with their application, all point to a structure built through human instrumentality - as distinct from Christ's Church (his Body, Ephesians 1:22,23) of Matthew 16 which Christ Himself builds. And the Apostle Paul's words in First Corinthians chapter 3 are consistent with those of Peter. When Paul addressed the Church of God at Corinth, he said: "... you are ... God's building. According to the grace of God which was given to me, like a wise master builder I laid a foundation, and another is building on it. But each man must be careful how he builds on it. For no man can lay a foundation other than the one which is laid, which is Jesus Christ" (1 Corinthians 3:9-11).

Paul's not talking about Christ's Church here, the Church the Body, which comprises all born-again believers – and which we've already heard from Scripture is built upon the rock. No, Paul's talking about the local church of God at Corinth. Notice that he, not Christ, is the builder. Paul says: "I laid a foundation ... like a wise master builder". This has got to be different, therefore, from the Church the Body about which Christ said: "I will build My church".

Paul might have been the wise master builder, but Christ Himself is still the foundation of each and every local church of God. The Apostle Paul laid the foundation by means of his teaching ministry. The constitutional basis of the local church according to the New Testament is the Apostles' teaching – which was Christ's own teaching delivered to them to pass on (Jude 3). In a very real sense the foundation on which we in turn are to build is Christ as identified with His own teaching. There's no other foundation which is according to God's Word. We must build on Christ on whom we first believed, and we must be careful how we build, for First Corinthians 3 goes on to tell us that our own building work will one day be tested by God to see if it's in accord with Christ, the stone of testing. So, Biblical thoughts of our believing on Christ and our building on Christ have moved us in thought from the imagery of a rock to that of a stone.

CHAPTER THREE: IN CHRIST (OUR INHERITANCE)

No other religion offers its adherents a personal union with its founder – by which means we may confidently, and yet humbly, claim to know God. Only Christianity offers this. In the previous chapter, we were thinking of the wonderful truth that by genuinely professing saving faith we enter into membership of Christ's Church (Matthew 16:18). This Church is what's known biblically as His, that's Christ's Body (Ephesians 1:21,22). When writing to the Corinthians in his first letter, chapter 12, Paul draws an analogy with the human body and he does it like this: "For even as the body is one and yet has many members, and all the members of the body, though they are many, are one body, so also is [lit. the] Christ" (1 Corinthians 12:12).

That reference to Christ is literally a reference to 'the Christ', apparently indicating 'the Church the Body of Christ' – being in the context of a verse all about members of the body. The Church here is identified with Christ – being in a mystical union with him: Head and body are one. This is what it means to be in Christ. It's one and the same as being in the body, Christ's Church. For Paul again says, and this time he's writing to the Romans (in chapter 12), "as in one body we have many members ... so we, though many, are one body in Christ" (Romans 12:4,5).

This emphasizes the fact that we're not only in relationship with Christ, but, of course, with all others who are also related with Him in his Church, his body. Our being 'in Christ' confronts us with the thrilling reality of our unity in the Body, a unity that's not only with Christ our head, but with all other believers also.

But, of course, through personal faith in the Lord Jesus, we enter into this relationship as individuals. Notice with me this personal dimension in Second Corinthians. It's there Paul speaks about knowing "a man in Christ" (2 Corinthians 12:1). That expression, "a man in Christ", stresses the personal union each believer knows with Christ. 'In Christ' means in union with Christ - as members of his body, the Church. You find the same thing at the end of Paul's letter to the Romans (Romans 16:7) when he's writing of various co-workers. Of a couple of them he tells us they were 'in Christ before me", which can only mean that they became Christian believers before Paul himself was converted. Once again, this is helpful as we confirm exactly what it means to be 'in Christ'.

Basically, the Bible clarifies that before we come to Jesus as saviour, we were dead 'in our sins'; upon believing we become alive 'in Christ'. Our status before God is either one of being 'in our sins' or 'in Christ' – and, we say again, we become a man or woman 'in Christ' through receiving Him by personal faith. Having said that, I feel I want to pause and remind you of the words Jesus Christ spoke to the Jews in his audience one day. He said: "Unless you believe that I am He, you will die in your sins" and then he said if you "die in your sin; where I am going, you cannot come" (John 8:24,21). How unspeakably solemn that is! And how tragic: to die and to be without Christ for all eternity. Tragic indeed, when God is still freely inviting us to come to His Son for salvation while there's time. But what's at stake is far more than being saved from a lost eternity. To be 'in Christ' brings with it a wealth of spiritual blessings. And I'd now like to explore these with you. Let's review some of them from Ephesians 1:

> "Blessed be the God and Father of our Lord Jesus Christ, who has blessed us with every spiritual blessing in the heavenly places in Christ, just as He chose us in Him before the foundation of the world, that we would

be holy and blameless before Him. In love He predestined us to adoption as sons through Jesus Christ to Himself, according to the kind intention of His will, to the praise of the glory of His grace, which He freely bestowed on us in the Beloved.

In Him we have redemption through His blood, the forgiveness of our trespasses, according to the riches of His grace which He lavished on us. In all wisdom and insight He made known to us the mystery of His will, according to His kind intention which He purposed in Him with a view to an administration suitable to the fullness of the times, that is, the summing up of all things in Christ, things in the heavens and things on the earth. In Him also we have obtained an inheritance, having been predestined according to His purpose who works all things after the counsel of His will, to the end that we who were the first to hope in Christ would be to the praise of His glory. In Him, you also, after listening to the message of truth, the gospel of your salvation - having also believed, you were sealed in Him with the Holy Spirit of promise, who is given as a pledge of our inheritance, with a view to the redemption of God's own possession, to the praise of His glory" (Ephesians 1:3-14).

In virtually every verse Jesus Christ is mentioned, and the blessings listed are ours by virtue of our being 'in Christ' (10 mentions!) – they come to us through the grace that God has freely bestowed on us in the Beloved, that is in Christ, for He's God's beloved Son. In Him, God has chosen, adopted, accepted, redeemed and forgiven us. And there's even more, as we read. For in Christ we've been given an inheritance, and to confirm that in advance, we've also been sealed in Christ with the Holy Spirit. All

who are in Christ have received the Holy Spirit. Paul says
elsewhere (Romans 8:9) "if anyone does not have the Spirit of
Christ, he does not belong to Him". It's good to know we belong,
and that this spiritual status of being 'in Christ' is ours. Having the
Holy Spirit is our assurance of these things. God has sealed us in
Christ with the Holy Spirit (2 Corinthians 1:22). We should
enjoy to the full the ring of confident assurance there is in that.

You can't be saved today, and then lost tomorrow. What God
does, he does forever (Ecclesiastes 3:14). The idea behind this
word for God having sealed us in Christ with His Holy Spirit, is
the idea of being stamped for the purpose of security. Believer,
God wants you to know that your salvation is secure. It came
through the grace of God, and it remains yours through his grace.
These great 'in Christ' blessings – every last one of them - are all
secure blessings.

So, in Christ we have obtained an inheritance, our text says.
This word is only used here in the New Testament, and it literally
meant to divide up land into allotted portions or lots. That's what
the tribes of Israel had to do in the promised land, but God's
provided something better for us. This assurance makes us ready to
join in saying with the apostle Peter:

> "Blessed be the God and Father of our Lord Jesus
> Christ, who according to His great mercy has caused us
> to be born again to a living hope through the
> resurrection of Jesus Christ from the dead, to obtain an
> inheritance which is imperishable and undefiled and
> will not fade away, reserved in heaven for you, who are
> protected by the power of God through faith for a
> salvation ready to be revealed in the last time. In this
> you greatly rejoice, even though now for a little while, if

necessary, you have been distressed by various trials" (1 Peter 1:3-6).

Our homeward journey can be difficult, but, as the hymn-writer has said, it would be worth it even though "seven deaths lay between". We rejoice together that God has been pleased to bless us with every spiritual blessing in the heavenly places in Christ. The fact that they're described as being "in the heavenly places" only serves to remind us that our Lord Jesus has been victorious over all "the spiritual forces of wickedness in the heavenly places" (Ephesians 6:12). Praise his name!

CHAPTER FOUR: UNDER CHRIST (OUR LORD)

The invitation of the Lord Jesus Christ is: "Come to Me, all who are weary and heavy-laden, and I will give you rest. Take My yoke upon you and learn from Me, for I am gentle and humble in heart, and YOU WILL FIND REST FOR YOUR SOULS. For My yoke is easy and My burden is light" (Matthew 11:28-30). The imagery Jesus uses is taken from the use of oxen, and so means to work for someone. The 'yoke' is the badge of (spiritual) service and is sometimes used in the Bible as a symbol of slavery (Leviticus 26:13); of afflictions (Lamentations 3:27); of the burden of sin (Lamentations 1:14); and of religious legalism (Acts 15:10; Galatians 5:1) with all its wearisome rituals. In other words, it always pictures something heavy, something hard to bear; something that's wearisome.

When Jesus used the imagery of the yoke here, the idea is that we should obey Him. It's the work of God that we should trust and obey him (see John 6:29). The restraints of His teaching are mild, gentle, and easy, compared with the burdensome laws and ceremonies of the Jews (see Acts 15:10) – and indeed compared with the religious duties of pagans. Jesus' yoke is easy. By contrast, it's sin that enslaves us. It's in John's Gospel that we find: "Jesus ... saying to those Jews who had believed Him, 'If you continue in My word, then you are truly disciples of Mine; and you will know the truth, and the truth will make you free...' ... [whereas] everyone who commits sin is the slave of sin" (John 8:31-34).

If we've known the saving power of Jesus Christ, then the thrust of the Apostle Paul's spiritual logic is vitally relevant to us, when, in Romans chapter 6, he talks of how we are to express the fact that we're under new management, saying:

> "... do not let sin reign in your mortal body so that you obey its lusts, and do not go on presenting the members of your body to sin as instruments of unrighteousness; but present yourselves to God as those alive from the dead, and your members as instruments of righteousness to God. For sin shall not be master over you, for you are not under law but under grace. What then? Shall we sin because we are not under law but under grace? May it never be! Do you not know that when you present yourselves to someone as slaves for obedience, you are slaves of the one whom you obey, either of sin resulting in death, or of obedience resulting in righteousness? But thanks be to God that though you were slaves of sin, you became obedient from the heart to that form of teaching to which you were committed, and having been freed from sin, you became slaves of righteousness" (Romans 6:12-18).

That last verse expresses clearly the idea of a change of yoke. The Lord takes away the yoke of the slavery of sin, and offers us instead His own gentle yoke. The idea of 'presenting ourselves to someone as slaves to obedience' is the idea of taking their yoke upon ourselves. As Christians, as followers of Jesus Christ, we're not to let sin have the lordship over our life. The reason for that is that having given our life to Christ, we're under new management. Jesus Christ is to have lordship over our lives. What Paul's just said comes hard on the heels of his teaching about believer's baptism. In actual fact, it's the practical outworking of that teaching.

Paul's just explained that baptism (by immersion) is a picture of death and resurrection implying a commitment to die to our old way of living and rise to the new life we already received when we believed in the Lord Jesus. As a result, we're to count ourselves as dead to sin and alive to God (Romans 6:11). Our water baptism is an important, biblical reminder that as followers of Christ, we've placed ourselves under His authority - under His yoke, with the expectation that we'll live out His teaching and serve Him. This brings us back to the idea of the yoke with which we began. It's clear then from all we've said that coming to Christ involves not only the removal of an ill-fitting yoke, but the taking of a new, well-fitted yoke. Again, we say that a yoke was – and in some places still is – placed on animals to harness them to something like a plough so that they might do service for the farmer. Those who come to Christ are to do so with the intention of following Him as disciples, going his way, under his authority in service for Him. Notice our Lord said: 'take My yoke upon you and learn of Me'. Our minds as well as our wills are to be under His easy yoke.

Christ described His yoke as 'easy' in the sense it's light; His are not grievous or burdensome commands – actually they are the best way to live (Romans 12:2)! But, from another angle, it's not 'easy', for authority is being challenged all around us today. The spirit of lawlessness, as the Bible predicted, is on the rise, it seems. Part of the challenge to authority comes when people assert their perceived rights to certain freedoms. The popular view is that you can't be 'set under authority' while experiencing true freedom at the same time – but that's exactly what Jesus Christ claimed is possible!

It's the claim of Christianity that both living under authority and living in freedom are possible at the same time - provided the authority in question is the authority of Jesus Christ. When once we recognize that Jesus is rightfully Lord, and we begin to appreciate the quality of His lordship, we soon discover a personal sense of true freedom while living under His authority. It's a freedom not to do as we please, but to do God's will in our lives – a freedom from the demands of our own self-will. We actually prove for ourselves that God's will is not only acceptable, but it's the best thing there is (Romans 12:2)! As Jesus promised, we find that the truth has set us free. We are truly free when we submit to Jesus' authority for He is rightfully Lord. Let's explore the quality of Jesus' lordship a bit further. After his resurrection, we're told that God had made His Son, Jesus, both Lord and Christ. He's now exalted above at the right-hand of God the Father. We're told:

> "God highly exalted Him, and bestowed on Him the name which is above every name, so that at the name of Jesus EVERY KNEE WILL BOW, of those who are in heaven and on earth and under the earth, and that every tongue will confess that Jesus Christ is Lord, to the glory of God the Father (Philippians 2:9-11).

The following similar words come from the Ephesians' letter chapter 1:19-23, where it talks about:

> "... the surpassing greatness of His power toward us who believe. These are in accordance with the working of the strength of His might which He brought about in Christ, when He raised Him from the dead and seated Him at His right hand in the heavenly places, far above all rule and authority and power and dominion, and every name that is named, not only in this age but also in the one to come. And He put all things in subjection under His feet, and gave Him as head over all things to the church, which is His body, the fullness of Him who fills all in all" (Ephesians 1:19-23).

That explains the basis for Jesus' rightful claim to be Lord over our lives. 'Jesus is Lord!' appears to have been a great confessional cry of the early Christians. Similar words are recorded three times in the New Testament. The early Christians appreciated the lordship of Christ and the spiritual freedom that went hand in hand with living under His authority - simply because when Christ is given His rightful place, everything else falls into place.

Let's pause to think about what it meant to those early Christians to say: 'Jesus is Lord'. "Confess ... Jesus as Lord ... [whom] God raised ... from the dead," Paul writes in Romans 10:9. In terms of understanding its full significance, the title 'Lord', as applied to Jesus, pivots upon His resurrection. For in the upper room Thomas joined with it the absolute title of deity: 'My Lord and my God'. Again, Paul reminds us, this time when writing to the Corinthians: "No-one can say "Jesus is Lord", except by the Holy Spirit" (1 Corinthians 12:3). It's true that our lives will only declare Christ's lordship through the Holy Spirit's working. The Biblical challenge is to take His yoke, learn from Him, and find rest in His service while giving Him the title role in our lives by the Spirit's help.

We've already quoted the third record of the early Christian cry confessing Jesus as Lord – that, you'll remember, was in Philippians chapter two: "every tongue will confess that Jesus Christ is Lord" (Philippians 2:11). There we learn that the lordship of Jesus Christ expresses itself in humility – after all we began by thinking of him as 'gentle and humble in heart.' When we have the same attitude, we'll be other-centred (Philippians 2:4); not status-seeking (v.6); we'll also be disinterested in position, power, prestige or privilege. It's amazing to think that the only place on earth where the Lord endorsed His title as 'Lord' was when he was on his knees: washing the disciples' feet (John 13:13). That's the secret why it's true freedom to submit our lives wholly under the authority of such a loving Lord who has served, and continues to serve, us so well!

CHAPTER FIVE: WITH CHRIST (OUR LIFE)

Many people nowadays tend to wear designer clothing sporting their favourite fashion designer label or celebrity name. In this way, they choose to identify with certain brands which are perhaps worn by the rich and famous. Others wear soccer shirts which boast the name of their team's latest star player. We like identifying with a winner. Some people have an addiction to so-called 'soap operas' - long-running serialized adaptations on TV of supposedly everyday-style dramas. For many it's become an obsession, which may be because it seems to allow its addicts to escape their own mundane reality and identify with the screen characters. The same thing bankrolls Hollywood. Other people identify themselves with a cause, some of them very noble causes which aim to tackle disease or poverty or injustice. Their association with the cause, or some organization relating to it, often comes to define their existence in some cases.

By reading what the Apostle Paul wrote in the Bible, it would seem no Christian ought to have an identity crisis. For Paul speaks about "our life ... with Christ" – Paul talks about our being identified with Christ at every stage of His saving career. What do I mean by that? Well, the Bible tells us that "Christ died for our sins, was buried and ... the third day rose again" (1 Corinthians 15:1-3). He was then "caught up to God and to his throne" (Revelation 12). These things – Christ's death, burial, resurrection and ascension - are not only historical realities, but they're presented to us in the Bible as having everyday meaning - for us - in our present experience. They're to define our lives in this world as we, as Christians, identify totally with Jesus Christ. We're to identify with Him to the extent of understanding biblically that He's our life! It's at least a five-stage identification as Paul outlines the fact that we died with Him; were buried with Him; were raised with Him; were seated with Him; and will be glorified with Him. We begin with Paul in Romans chapter 6, let's start at verse 1:

> "What shall we say then? Are we to continue in sin so that grace may increase? May it never be! How shall we who died to sin still live in it? Or do you not know that all of us who have been baptized into Christ Jesus have been baptized into His death? Therefore we have been buried with Him through baptism into death, so that as Christ was raised from the dead through the glory of the Father, so we too might walk in newness of life. For if we have become united with Him in the likeness of His death, certainly we shall also be in the likeness of His resurrection, knowing this, that our old self was crucified with Him, in order that our body of sin might be done away with, so that we would no longer be slaves to sin; for he who has died is freed from sin. Now if we have died with Christ, we believe that we shall also live with Him" (Romans 6:1-8).

This is believer's baptism in water that Paul's talking about as he talks about death, burial and resurrection. We could sum up Paul's message in this chapter as saying to each believer: 'you shouldn't live like you did before you knew Jesus, because you're not the person you once were'. When we trusted in Jesus for forgiveness, Paul tells us, our old or former self died. That former self was dominated by our corrupt human nature. Our new self, after conversion, possesses the new life Jesus gives to all who come to Him for forgiveness, and there's all the potential for our life now to be dominated by Jesus Christ instead of our corrupt human nature. Dying to our old way of life and rising to live in newness of life is the ambition that's pictured in the drama of water baptism for the follower of the Lord Jesus Christ.

Paul's still speaking about this topic as we turn now to his writing to the Colossians, he writes to them about their experience of:

> "having been buried with Him in baptism, in which [he says] you were also raised up with Him through faith in the working of God, who raised Him from the dead. When you were dead in your transgressions and the uncircumcision of your flesh, He made you alive together with Him, having forgiven us all our transgressions, having canceled out the certificate of debt consisting of decrees against us, which was hostile to us; and He has taken it out of the way, having nailed it to the cross" (Colossians 2:12-14).

That's covering the same points as in Romans chapter 6 about how when we turn to God, believing in His Son, Jesus, God sees us as having died with Christ and having been buried with him. In reality, our faith unites us with Christ, so that Christ's death was our death, and because of that, by God's grace, we're freed from the penalty of our sins by it. God took our bill of debt, nailed it to Christ's cross, and declared us free of all debt as a result. Isn't that wonderful? But there's more! For Paul's not finished yet:

> "Therefore if you have been raised up with Christ, keep seeking the things above, where Christ is, seated at the right hand of God. set your mind on the things above, not on the things that are on earth. For you have died and your life is hidden with Christ in God. When Christ, who is our life, is revealed, then you also will be revealed with Him in glory" (Colossians 3:1-4).

These words always remind me of an incident from my boyhood days. My old Bible teacher really wanted us to understand the way in which our life is 'hidden': hidden with Christ. I remember him telling us one particular Saturday how we were to handle enquiries at school the following Monday – enquiries about how we'd spent the weekend. 'When they ask you what you did on Saturday', he said, 'you'll tell them I was at a Young People's Meeting around the Bible. And they'll say to you: "Was that the best you could do? We went to the football match. What did you do on Sunday then?" And my old Bible teacher continued, 'you'll say: "I was remembering my Lord Jesus in a special church service designed for that purpose". And they'll say: "What a waste of time! We slept late then later on in the day we went to the cinema to watch a movie." "You can tell them", my old Bible teacher said – for he was determined to press home his point – "that you returned later to a church gathering where the good news about Jesus as Saviour was being preached." His point was that they couldn't possibly appreciate the quality of our hidden life with Christ. "But one day", he said, "when we're visibly glorified with Christ, they'll say: 'Ah, that's what made them tick!'"

But if in the meantime, as we wait for Christ's return, non-Christians don't understand and appreciate the spiritual nature and quality of our hidden life – our life which is already hidden with Christ in God; then it's also true that even some Christians – perhaps all of us at some time or other – don't always live in the enjoyment of it. The Bible reveals it as a spiritual reality: this fact that we're seated with Christ on high, but we need to have it as our mindset – we need to set our minds on things above. Too easily, we get bogged down in things below, on this earth, among the clutter of our daily lives. There was a man won a free return ticket for an Atlantic crossing on a luxury liner. He was poor, and decided to take dried biscuits and cheese in a plastic bag to live on for the whole crossing. He was content to eat his meagre fare while the others dined in the fancy restaurants, because he was just so glad to be on the trip of a lifetime. When nearly home, he thought he'd try just one last meal in the high-class restaurant. He cautiously asked the waiter the price. The waiter was astonished: had he not read his ticket? All the meals were included!

In granting to the believer an afterlife that's guaranteed, God's also included everything we need for life in all its fullness which includes strength to cope with the trials of life; having a wonderful sense of purpose and direction in life; with the supernatural ability to find joy in the strangest of places; and best of all unending personal encouragement and companionship with the Lord here and now – but we've got to read the ticket! We've got to set our minds on the things above, the things which are consistent with his glory upon heaven's throne. Our lives need to resemble lives of sons of the great King!

And nothing, absolutely nothing, can separate us from the love of God which is in Christ Jesus our Lord (Romans 8:39), for if we die before our Lord should return, we have Paul's assurance to rely on when he wrote from the prison-house to his Philippian friends to tell them:

> "according to my earnest expectation and hope … Christ will even now, as always, be exalted in my body, whether by life or by death … I do not know which to choose. But I am hard-pressed from both directions, having the desire to depart and be with Christ, for that is very much better" (Philippians 1:20-23).

This reveals to us that the soul of a believer who dies in this age of grace goes at once to be 'with Christ'. So, we're identified with him in this life, and at home with him when it ends! Praise the Lord!

CHAPTER SIX: UNTO CHRIST (OUR MASTER & JUDGE)

If there's one theme that's meant to integrate every aspect of our lives, surely it must be this: that whatever we do we're to do it as unto the Lord Jesus. We often tend to divide our life up into various compartments. We think of our church life, our work or business life, and beyond that, our life in the world in general. In each of these contexts we've different sets of responsibilities – but there's one thing in common over all: in every case our primary responsibility is to our Lord Jesus Christ. It's the Lord whom we serve 24/7 – twenty-four hours a day, seven days a week.

In each of the areas we've mentioned we often have challenging responsibilities. Let's take first of all our church life. Inevitably, different opinions will arise on minor matters of detail in relation to practical service and personal preference. The apostle Paul illustrates how we're to handle this from a first century case study drawn from the situation of his friends in the church at Rome. Let's check out how Paul emphasizes our responsibility to show respect for others and their views. The particular issue two thousand years ago concerned criss-crossing tensions in the church. Reading between the lines, it would seem that those who'd come to faith from a Jewish background had a special sensitivity about what they saw as others abusing the Jewish high and holy days which they'd previously observed as part of the Law of Moses. On the other hand, those from a formerly pagan background were suspicious about eating meat from the meat-markets. This was because they'd previously been accustomed to such meat ending up there after having been used in rituals involving animal sacrifice to the pagan gods. So, there were these opposing sets of sensitivities. In Romans chapter 14, we discover how the Holy Spirit directed Paul in the counsel he gave. He urged them to:

> "Receive one who is weak in the faith, but not to disputes over doubtful things. For one believes he may eat all things, but he who is weak eats only vegetables. Let not him who eats despise him who does not eat, and let not him who does not eat judge him who eats; for God has received him. Who are you to judge another's servant? To his own master he stands or falls. Indeed, he will be made to stand, for God is able to make him stand. One person esteems one day above another; another esteems every day alike.
>
> Let each be fully convinced in his own mind. He who observes the day, observes it to the Lord; and he who does not observe the day, to the Lord he does not observe it. He who eats, eats to the Lord, for he gives God thanks; and he who does not eat, to the Lord he does not eat, and gives God thanks. For none of us lives to himself, and no one dies to himself. For if we live, we live to the Lord; and if we die, we die to the Lord. Therefore, whether we live or die, we are the Lord's. For to this end Christ died and rose and lived again, that He might be Lord of both the dead and the living. But why do you judge your brother? Or why do you show contempt for your brother? For we shall all stand before the judgment seat of Christ" (Romans 14:1-10).

In these matters of legitimate differences of view, neither party was to treat the other with contempt. Each was to get on with doing what they were fully convinced of, and to do it as '(un)to the Lord'. Different opinions and different practices regarding observing certain days or eating specific foods would remain, but what brought it all into harmony was the over-riding principle of each believer doing what he or she did as genuinely 'unto the Lord'. That demonstrates our primary responsibility in each and every situation - which is our responsibility to the Lord. Take next our business life, or our work situation. For most of us, things are quite a bit different to what they were like in the workplace two thousand years ago. But the principle is still the same. When we read about slaves and masters, we can think of employees and employers. It's in Colossians chapter 3 that Paul has this to say:

> "Bondservants, obey in all things your masters according to the flesh, not with eyeservice, as men-pleasers, but in sincerity of heart, fearing God. And whatever you do, do it heartily, as to the Lord and not to men, knowing that from the Lord you will receive the reward of the inheritance; for you serve the Lord Christ. But he who does wrong will be repaid for what he has done, and there is no partiality. Masters, give your bondservants what is just and fair, knowing that you also have a Master in heaven" (Colossians 3:22-4:1).

At work our responsibility extends beyond doing the right thing when the boss is watching, and it extends beyond simply keeping the company happy. I once remember reading about a servant girl, who'd been asked how she knew she was a converted Christian – what difference had it made in her life? She replied: "Well, you see, I used to sweep the dust under the mat, but now I don't." Yes, it's possible to sweep a room as if Jesus Christ were going to visit it; or to type a letter as if it were addressed to the Lord Jesus; or cook a meal as if Christ were to eat it; or serve a customer as if Jesus were that shopper; and so on. As Paul says: "whatever you do, do it heartily, as to the Lord". Even in our secular employment our primary responsibility is to the Lord Jesus Christ.

Then there's our responsibility to the world at large; a world which is often a needy world. Perhaps we can learn the principle here from the Lord's words describing his return to the earth at the time of the end. He predicted:

> "When the Son of Man comes in His glory, and all the holy angels with Him, then He will sit on the throne of His glory. All the nations will be gathered before Him, and He will separate them one from another, as a shepherd divides his sheep from the goats. And He will set the sheep on His right hand, but the goats on the left. Then the King will say to those on His right hand, 'Come, you blessed of My Father, inherit the kingdom prepared for you from the foundation of the world: for I was hungry and you gave Me food; I was thirsty and you gave Me drink; I was a stranger and you took Me in; I was naked and you clothed Me; I was sick and you visited Me; I was in prison and you came to Me.'

> "Then the righteous will answer Him, saying, 'Lord, when did we see You hungry and feed You, or thirsty and give You drink? When did we see You a stranger and take You in, or naked and clothe You? Or when did we see You sick, or in prison, and come to You?' And the King will answer and say to them, 'Assuredly, I say to you, inasmuch as you did it to one of the least of these My brethren, you did it to Me.' Then He will also say to those on the left hand, 'Depart from Me, you cursed, into the everlasting fire prepared for the devil and his angels: for I was hungry and you gave Me no food; I was thirsty and you gave Me no drink; I was a stranger and

you did not take Me in, naked and you did not clothe
Me, sick and in prison and you did not visit Me.' Then
they also will answer Him, saying, 'Lord, when did we
see You hungry or thirsty or a stranger or naked or sick
or in prison, and did not minister to You?' "Then He
will answer them, saying, 'Assuredly, I say to you,
inasmuch as you did not do it to one of the least of
these, you did not do it to Me. And these will go away
into everlasting punishment, but the righteous into
eternal life" (Matthew 25:31-46).

The setting of this scene is the Lord's judgement of the nations
which will be alive on the earth at the time of his return to set up
his thousand-year reign on this earth. But we shouldn't be lulled
into thinking good works will save us or anyone else. The Bible
consistently proclaims we're justified by faith in Christ; however,
good works – even of the simplest kind – are the public evidence
of that personal and private faith which saves us. We can be
challenged in this by the example of some who have ministered
selflessly to people poorer and more ill than themselves – having
done so in the attitude that they were ministering to Christ
himself. Perhaps, we each need to consider if such a thought might
transform a relationship we're currently struggling with, or a duty
we're complaining about. In every part of our lives, and with
whoever it is we're relating to, let's be reminded that whatever we
do is unto the Lord.

CHAPTER SEVEN: FOR CHRIST (OUR LOVER)

During the second World War, on the last day of July 1941, the sirens in a German prisoner-of-war camp (Auschwitz) sounded to announce the escape of a prisoner. In revenge, ten of his fellow prisoners were to be sentenced to death by starvation while buried alive in a specially constructed, concrete bunker. All day, tortured by sun, hunger and fear, the men waited as the German commandant and his Gestapo assistant walked between the ranks to select - totally at random - the chosen ten. As the commandant pointed to one man whose name was Francis Gajowniczek, he cried out in despair, 'My poor wife and children'. At that moment, the unimpressive figure of a man with sunken eyes and round glasses in wire frames stepped out of line and took off his cap.

What does this Polish pig want?' asked the commandant. 'I am a Catholic priest; I want to die for that man. I am old, he has a wife and children ... I have no one,' said Father Maximilian Kolbe. 'Accepted', retorted the commandant, and moved on. That night, nine men and one priest went to the starvation cell. Normally, they would tear each other apart like cannibals – but not this time. While they had strength, lying naked on the floor, the men prayed and sang hymns. After two weeks, three of the men and Father Maximilian were still alive. The bunker was required for others, so on the 14th of August, the remaining four were disposed of. At 12:50 pm, after two weeks in the starvation bunker and still conscious, the Polish priest was finally given an injection of phenol and died at the age of forty-seven.

On 10 October 1982 in St. Peter's Square, Rome, Father Maximilian's death was honoured. Present in the crowd of 150,000 was Francis Gajowniczek, his wife, his children, and his children's children – for indeed, many had been saved by that one man. That's a true and moving story with the power to inspire others to acts of sacrificial love. The Bible tells us: "... for the good man someone would dare even to die. But God demonstrates His own love toward us, in that while we were yet sinners, Christ died for us" (Romans 5:7,8).

The death of Jesus Christ was different. He died for us while we were still enemies – while we were still hostile to Him. The apostle Paul writes further in 2 Corinthians 5:14,15 of how that thought should move us to action and motivate all our service for him. He wrote: "For the love of Christ controls us, having concluded this, that one died for all, therefore all died; and He died for all, so that they who live might no longer live for themselves, but for Him who died and rose again on their behalf". In reminding us of our obligation to live for the one who died for us, Paul uses some quite graphic language. The same word which is rendered here as 'controls' as in 'the love of Christ controls us' crops up in expressions like 'gripped with a fever' (so Doctor Luke uses it in Luke 4:38; Acts 28:8). It seems clear that the idea is that in the same way that a body is gripped by a fever, so our hearts and lives are to be gripped by an appreciation of what the Lord, in love, has done for us - gripped by the power of His mighty love which led Him to sacrifice Himself for us.

There's an irresistible logic in what Paul's saying. Let's hear it again: "For the love of Christ controls us, having concluded this, that one died for all, therefore all died; and He died for all, so that they who live might no longer live for themselves, but for Him who died and rose again on their behalf" (2 Corinthians 5:14,15). Notice the word: 'therefore'. The reasoning is, we say, as irresistible as it's clear: Christ died, and we died with Him - since we are united with Him by faith. Then Christ was raised, and so we are to live for Him and not for ourselves. That's the supreme motivation by which we are to serve - and even suffer if need be – for Christ.

Later in the same chapter, just a few verses further on, Paul expands on exactly how we're to live for the Lord. He tells us we're to be ambassadors for Him. He says God has committed to us the word of reconciliation and "Therefore, we are ambassadors for Christ, as though God were making an appeal through us; we beg you on behalf of Christ, be reconciled to God" (2 Corinthians 5:20). Of course, we know that an ambassador is a minister of the highest rank, employed by one sovereign state at the court of another, to represent the dignity and power of his sovereign (Webster). He's sent to do what the sovereign would do if he himself were present. An ambassador is bound to obey the instructions of his or her sovereign. As far as possible, an ambassador does only what the sovereign would do if he himself were present. We're to be ambassadors for Christ, having been sent to do what He would do if He were personally present. That's some thought, isn't it, as we remember how our sovereign Lord went about doing good and preaching the good news of God's kingdom.

Like Christ, we're to explain the terms on which God is willing to be reconciled to people. As with any ambassador, we're not to negotiate new terms, nor follow our own plans, but simply to seek the honor of the sovereign who's sent us, and to seek only His will. In the measure we're true ambassadors, we'll not be about the business of promoting our own well-being; only occupied with the business which the Son of God Himself would engage in were He again personally on the earth. One example, if I may, comes to mind ...

C.T. Studd (1860-1931) was an English missionary who selflessly served his Saviour in China, India, and Africa. His motto was: 'If Jesus Christ is God and died for me, then no sacrifice can be too great for me to make for Him.' These were the words of a man motivated by the great love of Christ we have been hearing about – so motivated as to become a bold ambassador for Him. Charles Thomas Studd was born in England in 1860, one of three sons of a wealthy retired planter, Edward Studd, who had made a fortune in India and had come back to England to spend it. After being converted to Christ (during a Moody-Sankey campaign in England in 1877), he became deeply concerned about the spiritual welfare of his three sons and influenced them for the cause of Christ before his death two years later.

By the time C.T. was sixteen he had become an expert cricket player and at nineteen was captain of his team at Eton College. He was further educated at Trinity College, Cambridge, where he was also recognized as an outstanding cricketer. C.T. was saved in 1878 at the age of 18 when a visiting preacher at their home caught C.T. on his way to play cricket. 'Are you a Christian?' he asked. C.T's answer was obviously not convincing enough, and so the guest pressed the point, and C.T. later testified: "I got down on my knees and I did say 'thank you' to God. And right then and there, joy and peace came into my soul. I knew then what it was to be 'born again,' and the Bible which had been so dry to me before, became everything." But as C.T. himself relates: 'Instead of going and telling others of the love of Christ, I was selfish and kept the knowledge to myself. The result was that gradually my love began to grow cold, and the love of the world began to come in. I spent six years in that unhappy backslidden state.'

But the Lord in his goodness worked in C.T.'s life and set him to work for Him, and to go to China as one of 'The Cambridge Seven' who offered themselves to Hudson Taylor for missionary service in the China Inland Mission (in February, 1885). China, then India, and finally the heart of Africa were the areas where he continued to work until his death in 1931. In Africa, he endured weakness and sickness; losing most of his teeth and suffering several heart attacks.

Well, we were talking about Christ's great love for us being the motivating factor in all our service for Him. Someone has spoken about the love of Christ being our 'magnificent obsession', the glorious impetus in all our serving for Him – service which may for us also (as for C.T. Studd), at times, involve suffering hardship for Christ's sake, as Paul wrote to his Christian friends in Philippi saying: "conduct yourselves in a manner worthy of the gospel of Christ ... with one mind striving together for the faith of the gospel ... For to you it has been granted for Christ's sake, not only to believe in Him, but also to suffer for His sake" (Philippians 1:27-29).

If Jesus Christ be God, and died for us, will we not live for Him, will we not be an ambassador for Him, and even be prepared to suffer for Him? Surely His love compels us!

CHAPTER EIGHT: OF CHRIST (OUR MODEL)

Perhaps you've heard the story that's told about the little girl who was drawing a picture. Her mother asked her: "What are you doing?" "I'm drawing a picture of God", she announced very matter of factly. "Don't be silly. No one knows what Gods looks like!" was her mother's reply. Unconcerned by this dampener, and without looking up, the girl simply replied: "Well, they will do by the time I've finished!" A child's innocence can sometimes give us food for thought. And perhaps this is another case in point. For there's a real sense in which our chief business as Christians is to give this world a picture of God. Our lives are to show to those around us what God is like. The way the Bible puts it is that we're to reflect God's glory. It says: "... we all, with unveiled face, beholding [or reflecting] as in a mirror the glory of the Lord, are being transformed into the same image from glory to glory, just as from the Lord, the Spirit" (2 Corinthians 3:18).

That's talking about the image of Christ, or our being changed into the likeness of Christ. The contrast Paul was making when he wrote this was with Moses whose face shone with a reflected glory when he emerged from the presence of God after one of his Old Testament mountain-top experiences. Whenever Moses went into the presence of God he removed the veil which covered his face, and his face was again illumined with his being in God's presence. As a result, Moses' face later shone when he delivered God's message to the people. Then, after the delivery of the message, and during his ordinary association with the people, he again kept his face covered (see Exodus 34:29-35).

In other words, his face for a while mirrored God's glory. Moses mirrored God's glory; we, too, are to mirror or reflect the glory of the Lord. But Moses, or at least the skin of his face, lost that glory – it needed to be 'recharged' by the next encounter with God. Now, here's the main contrast - it's not to be like that with us. Rather than losing the glory, we're to be continuously changed from glory to glory, from one glorious degree to another – it's to be an ever-increasing glory – as we're transformed into the same image: the glorious image of our Lord, He who on earth showed himself to be full of grace and truth. "Put on the new self, [Paul says when writing to the Ephesian Christians] which in the likeness of God has been created in righteousness and holiness of the truth" (Ephesians 4:24).

Is there any likeness of Christ visible in the holiness of my life in terms of practical righteousness? There should be. I often feel ashamed when I remember another story involving a child. It's the one where a missionary was telling children about the Lord Jesus. One child in the group grew quite excited as the missionary described the lovely character of the Lord Jesus. 'I know him', the child cried out, 'he lives down my street!' It would seem that a Christian, a follower of Christ, had been effectively mirroring the glory of his Lord in that neighbourhood. May this example of someone exhibiting the likeness of Christ be a challenge to our hearts. For it's certainly God's intention that we become like Christ because our new self has been created in righteousness and holiness of the truth. When Christ was here, God the Father spoke from heaven and said: "This is My beloved Son in whom I am well-pleased". God loves His Son so much, he wants us to be like Him. The Bible tells us that it's God's plan that we "become conformed to the image of his Son" (Romans 8:29).

One day, we'll be completely "like him, for we shall see him as he is", the apostle John assures us (1 John 3:1). At Christ's return, we'll not only be fully conformed to Christ in character, but our body also will be changed. Paul said as much to those in the first century Church of God in Corinth:

> "So also it is written, "The first MAN, Adam, BECAME A LIVING SOUL." The last Adam became a life-giving spirit. However, the spiritual is not first, but the natural; then the spiritual. The first man is from the earth, earthy; the second man is from heaven. As is the earthy, so also are those who are earthy; and as is the heavenly, so also are those who are heavenly. Just as we have borne the image of the earthy, we will also bear the image of the heavenly" (1 Corinthians 15:49).

The 'last Adam' and 'the second man', 'the man from heaven' are all pointers to Jesus, of course. With this statement to the Corinthians which tells us we'll bear the image of the heavenly, Paul's words in Philippians 3:21 agree, giving us the further wonderful detail that our new body will be like Christ's own 'glorious body'. However, despite the fact that this is our destiny: even to be fully conformed to the image of God's Son, so often in this intervening time while we wait for Him, the character we display, sadly, falls far short. A Hindu educationalist once said to an audience he was addressing: 'I see that a good many of you are Christians. Now this is not a religious lecture, but I'd like to pause long enough to say that if you Christians would live like Jesus Christ, India would be at your feet tomorrow' (from The Christ of the Indian Road by Stanley Jones, 1925).

While we wait for Christ, loving the one whom we've not yet seen, God's intention is that our ordinary, day-to-day lives should express the life of Christ. When the apostle Paul wrote a second time to his Corinthian friends, he had this to say:

"God, who said, "Light shall shine out of darkness," is the One who has shone in our hearts to give the Light of the knowledge of the glory of God in the face of Christ. But we have this treasure in earthen vessels, so that the surpassing greatness of the power will be of God and not from ourselves; we are afflicted in every way, but not crushed; perplexed, but not despairing; persecuted, but not forsaken; struck down, but not destroyed; always carrying about in the body the dying of Jesus, so that the life of Jesus also may be manifested in our body. For we who live are constantly being delivered over to death for Jesus' sake, so that the life of Jesus also may be manifested in our mortal flesh" (2 Corinthians 4:6-11).

Notice the repetition: 'that the life of Jesus ... may be manifested' in us. Is this not the treasure which we have in these earthen vessels, these jars of clay, which are our mortal bodies? This treasure is in all those who've been divinely enlightened to recognize the glory of God in the face of Jesus Christ. Just as the dying of Jesus was the means by which His powerful resurrection life could be part of our experience (Philippians 3:10), so trials and difficulties are often God's means of allowing the life of Jesus to become visible to others in and through us.

There seems here to be a reference back to the time of the Bible book of the Judges when God's ancient people, Israel, was afflicted, perplexed, persecuted and struck down at the hands of their Midianite enemies. But God raised up a man called Gideon, who at the head of only 300 men, and in much human weakness, experienced the greatness of the power of God in achieving a great victory. They went against the enemy at night armed only with swords and flaming torches hidden in clay jars. Those earthen vessels were suddenly broken to let the light shine out from the torches concealed inside them. It was a successful surprise attack in the dark. Now in this dark world God intends that we let the light and life of Jesus shine out in the surrounding spiritual darkness. Our own pride and wills need to be broken so that it's truly the life of Jesus that's seen in us. God wants the life of His Son to be seen in us.

God intends to make us more like Christ. He calls us to be imitators of Christ. How can we do that? We can imitate Christ by living a life of love. That's what the apostle Paul asked the Ephesians to do in chapter 5 of his letter to them: "Therefore be imitators of God, as beloved children; and walk in love, just as Christ also loved you and gave Himself up for us, an offering and a sacrifice to God as a fragrant aroma" (Ephesians 5:1). It was a message he repeated to the Corinthians: "Be imitators of me, just as I also am of Christ" (1 Corinthians 11:1).

May God help us to be true image-bearers of Christ, as we yield our bodies so that the life of Jesus can be seen in them, all the while making it our aim to become better imitators of Him.

BONUS CHAPTER ONE: ONE THING I KNOW

It's always impressive to see the degree of focus competing athletes have. Whether it's Jonathan Edwards in the triple jump, Usain Bolt going for gold in the 200 metres or Lionel Messi aiming to steer his Argentinian side to triumph in a World Cup final, we can read the same facial expressions that signal complete focus on the job in hand. I also get that same impression when I read about some people in the Bible. I get the feeling that they, too, had a real focus in their lives. Let me introduce you to the first of the ones I've selected. We find him in John's Gospel chapter 9. He's a man who started life with a disadvantage: he was born blind. But with his personal experience of going from minus to pus, he became an inspiring example of a very focused witness when he later testified to having experienced the power of Jesus Christ at first-hand. The Gospel writer, John, takes up the story:

> "Now as Jesus passed by, He saw a man who was blind from birth ... He spat on the ground and made day with the saliva; and He anointed the eyes of the blind man with the clay. And He said to him, "Go, wash in the pool of Siloam"... So he went and washed, and came back seeing. Therefore the neighbors and those who previously had seen that he was blind said, "Is not this he who sat and begged?" Some said, "This is he." Others said, "He is like him." He said, "I am he." Therefore they

said to him, "How were your eyes opened?" He answered and said, "A Man called Jesus made clay and anointed my eyes and said to me, 'Go to the pool of Siloam and wash.' So I went and washed, and I received sight"...

... they again called the man who was blind, and said to him, "Give God the glory! We know that this Man is a sinner." He answered and said, "Whether He is a sinner or not I do not know. One thing I know: that though I was blind, now I see." Then they said to him again, "What did He do to you? How did He open your eyes?" He answered them, "I told you already, and you did not listen. Why do you want to hear it again? Do you also want to become His disciples?" Then they reviled him and said, "You are His disciple, but we are Moses' disciples. "We know that God spoke to Moses; as for this fellow, we do not know where He is from." The man answered and said to them, "Why, this is a marvelous thing, that you do not know where He is from; yet He has opened my eyes! "Now we know that God does not hear sinners; but if anyone is a worshiper of God and does His will, He hears him. Since the world began it has been unheard of that anyone opened the eyes of one who was born blind. If this Man were not from God, He could do nothing." They answered and said to him, "You were completely born in sins, and are you teaching us?" And they cast him out Jesus heard that they had cast him out; and when He had found him, He said to him, "Do you believe in the Son of God?" He answered and said, "Who is He, Lord, that I may believe in Him?" And Jesus said to him, "You have both seen Him and it is He who is taking with you."

Then he said, "Lord, I believe!" And he worshiped Him" (John 9:1--38).

This unnamed disciple is an inspiration to us all. I'm sure there are times when we all struggle to witness. Some might think, "I don't know enough. If I were to speak up and declare my faith in Jesus, someone might ask me a question - and I probably wouldn't know how to answer it." Well, think about this. The man we've been hearing about was a brand-new disciple. His knowledge of Jesus was virtually non-existent. But this incident - with his witness - is included in our Bibles as an example of effective witnessing for Jesus Christ!

This man who had been born blind was someone who could testify to God's amazing grace in his life - the same as in John Newton's famous hymn,

"Amazing grace, how sweet the sound

That saved a wretch like me,

I once was lost, but now am found

Was blind, but now I see."

That sums up the testimony of this man in John chapter 9 in a physical, as well as spiritual, sense. Yet when the religious leaders came calling, it seems he felt he couldn't cope with their theological arguments, as they interrogated him about his encounter with Jesus. What he realized, however, and used to good effect, was the fact that people can't argue successfully against a real personal experience. After all, we ought to know what's happened to ourselves better than anyone else does. And so it was with this man. He didn't even know the very basics about Jesus, but his answer to the sceptics was, "One thing I know: that thought I was blind, now I see."

This was something he really was sure about. He had known this life-changing experience, so it became the focus of his witness. This was his 'one thing': 'one thing I know'. It's the kind of powerful testimony from experience that even the newest child of God can give. As believers, we've all got a story to tell: an experience of going from minus to plus - one which the drawing power of God can use to convince others. We can share with others how our life has changed: how God's grace has replaced our guilt; and how forgiveness has replaced failure and fear.

And we all have a responsibility to witness; each in our own way. One of the first ever Christian disciples was Andrew. It was he who brought his brother, Peter, to Jesus. Then, it was Andrew again who introduced the lad with the five loaves and two fish to Jesus on the day Jesus used them to feed more than five thousand people in the desert. If we can introduce a gospel leaflet into a friendly conversation, or invite a contact to a church service where God's Word will be preached, then we've done a service for God. After all, it's God's Spirit through God's Word, the Bible, that brings about conviction. Our job is just to introduce people to God's Word in a relevant way.

Andrew's brother, Peter, was a quite different character to Andrew. Peter was up-front and direct. Sometimes it's appropriate to be a bit provocative, to take a somewhat confrontational approach. But you may feel you're not suited for that - being more at home with the approach where you first build up a relationship of trust and respect in ordinary everyday things. That relationship, when built, can act like a bridge to drive home the Gospel in due course.

The apostle Paul loved to reason and persuade - debating with worldly-wise philosophers at Athens - in that great university centre of learning. When he was there he quoted the literature of their own culture, but at other times, when engaging devout Jews in debate, he drew on the Scriptures in which they were steeped. It was altogether different with Dorcas. She was skilled with her hands. She let her hands do the talking. The good works she did for others were an eloquent testimony. Long ago, someone said, "Preach the Gospel and, if necessary, use words." You may think that's going a bit far, but I hope you get the point.

Matthew, again one of the first twelve disciples, also seemed to have a quiet way with him. He's recorded in the Bible as saying little or nothing, but he was ready to open his house to colleagues so that they might come for a meal there with Jesus. There are lots of different ways to witness. It's not your style, but your focus, that counts. When we are in conversation with non-Christians about spiritual matters, let's be sure to stick to the one, main point: our personal conviction about the person of Jesus Christ. When did we last share with someone the 'one thing we know' that could make an eternal difference in their lives?

BONUS CHAPTER TWO: ONE THING I NEED

We're talking about having a 'focus' in our lives, the kind of focus that all top athletes. They could never get to the top if they didn't focus on improving their 'personal best'. To have a focus like that demands that we set priorities, and give major time to the things that really matter most to achieving our goal. The same thing applies if our goal is a spiritual one rather than a physical one. A spiritual goal may be improving our relationship with the Lord. It will demand time for us to get to know Him better. Other legitimate things in life may have to be sacrificed, or at least soft-pedaled. Having said that, it's hard to get the balance, isn't it, amid the pressures of studies, child-rearing, business, and an eagerness to be up and doing for the Lord? Those kinds of considerations set the scene for introducing someone we meet in Luke's Gospel, chapter 10. We'll let Luke take up the story, as he follows Jesus' progress towards Jerusalem and the cross:

> "Now it happened as they went that He entered a certain village; and a certain woman named Martha welcomed Him into her house. And she had a sister called Mary, who also sat at Jesus' feet and heard His word. But Martha was distracted with much serving, and she approached Him and said, "Lord, do You not care that my sister has left me to serve alone? Therefore tell her to help me." And Jesus answered and said to her, "Martha, Martha, you are worried and troubled about many things. But one thing is needed, and Mary has

chosen that good part, which will not be taken away from her'" (Luke 10:38-42).

Very often those who refer to this story are quite hard on Martha. But I can sympathize a lot with her. She certainly wasn't someone who always got it wrong. John records in his Gospel (chapter 12) on another occasion that 'Martha served'. That time there was no rebuke, for, of course, the Lord does want our service too. In fact, even in Luke's story, I think we've every reason to believe that Martha started well. We read that 'Martha was distracted with much serving'. The use of the word 'distracted' by Luke seems to imply that Martha had started out with her focus on Jesus Himself. What's more, it says she had a "sister called Mary, who also sat at Jesus' feet and heard his word." At least one way of reading that is to understand that Martha also had the habit of sitting and listening to Jesus.

So, on this occasion, Martha has been distracted by the fact that she had so many other things to do. Can you relate to that? I certainly can. How many things are on your 'to do' list for today? Someone else has described what's going on in situations like this one Martha was in as 'the tyranny of the to do list'. It's that list of things demanding our urgent attention as the day stretches before us. Yet isn't it so often when we've soft-pedalled on our quiet time that we, like Martha, become 'troubled about many things'? These words describe a state of inner turmoil: it's when we're in such a condition of inner agitation that we know the difference between a door being shut and a door being shut too loudly.

If we're wise, we'll recognize our own symptoms of overload, and how we tend to behave under stress. In a state like this, one thing quickly leads to another, and on to a demanding spirit. "Lord ... tell her to help me," Martha said. When tired and stressed, it's all too easy for us to become critical of others around us. But Martha did, at least, take her complaint to the Lord. And from the Lord that day she learnt there was 'one thing' she needed above and before everything else in her life. That 'one thing' was time in the Master's presence.

We agree wholeheartedly, of course. We nod and say, "That's right," but how can we actually achieve it, with all the noise and pace of modern life around us? Surely, the Lord's words, as always, contain the answer. He said: "Mary has chosen the good part." With these words, the Lord seems to be indicating that Mary had made a deliberate lifestyle choice. More and more often, it seems, we're being advised of a need to review our lifestyle. A patient presents a list of symptoms to her GP - only to be told that many of them could well be stress-related and so the conversation shifts to analysing her lifestyle: with questions about how much is packed into a day, into a week, into a month.

Establishments known as 'Health Farms' have become fashionable and offer clients a 'lifestyle makeover'. At some time, Mary had presumably had a lifestyle makeover. As a matter of deliberate choice, she'd 'chosen the good part.' That investment in 'the good part', for which the Lord commended her in Luke 10, led to the Lord again commending her for the actual service (the 'good work') that flowed from it in Matthew 26:

> "When Jesus was in Bethany at the house of Simon the leper, a woman came to Him having an alabaster flask of very costly fragrant oil, and she poured it on His head as He sat at the table. But when His disciples saw it, they were indignant, saying, "Why this waste? For this fragrant oil might have been sold for much and given to the poor." But when Jesus was aware of it, He said to them, "Why do you trouble the woman? For she has done a good work for Me. For you have the poor with

you always, but Me you do not have always. For in pouring this fragrant oil on My body, she did it for My burial. Assuredly, I say to you, wherever this gospel is preached in the whole world, what this woman has done will also be told as a memorial to her'" (Matthew 26:6--10).

By the way, this is the time when John, in his version of events (in chapter 12), tells us that Martha was also serving the Lord acceptably. Yet differing lifestyle choices were still revealed that day, too. Once again, Mary was at the receiving end of the critical comments of her fellow-disciples. For, as Mary lavished the expensive fragrance on Jesus, other disciples grumbled about the monetary value that had been wasted, as they perceived it. It was as if they couldn't see beyond material things. But what's the net worth of the things we hoard for ourselves? On the other hand, can there be any loss involved in dedicating whatever is valuable to the service of the Lord Jesus Christ? There's nothing more valuable than our time.

You've got to admire the focus that Mary had. Her focus was on the Lord. She was in tune with His wishes. You and I may know contemporary Christians like that, too: men and women who are outstanding for the focus they maintain on their relationship with the Lord Himself, often in the midst of busy lives of service.

There's no way this would be unwelcome attention! For the Lord himself invites us to have this focus on Himself. We're given a picture of Him in our Bibles standing at the door of hearts, knocking: "Behold, I stand at the door and knock. If anyone hears my voice and opens the door, I will come in to him and dine with him, and he with Me" (Revelation 3:20).

That's a very realistic picture for us, too, whenever our crowded lives threaten to leave Him on the outside. Sometimes we may keep Him knocking while a whole host of other things occupies our attention. Still the promise the Lord left for his disciples almost two thousand years ago remains for us to make our own today: "If anyone loves Me, [Jesus said] he will keep My word; and My Father will love him, and We will come to him and make Our home with him" (John 14:23).

I'm reminded of the story of an old professor who was very much at home with the Lord in his life - and the Lord at home with him. Two of his young students wanted to find out what their old professor did of an evening. So one day they sneaked into his study and hid and waited there. After his meal the old professor retired to his study, unaware, of course, that he was being observed by his students hiding in the room. The students watched as the old man sat down at his desk and got his Bible out along with his study books. At the end of the evening, they watched as the old man bowed his head in his hands and was heard to say, "Lord, there's nothing between."

He'd evidently allowed God's Word to search his heart and, unaware of any particular sin remaining on his conscience that day, he'd said, "Lord, there's nothing between." Nothing between. You can't get closer than that, can you? That's intimacy; intimacy with the Lord, by practising His presence. Notice how the old man did it. He read and studied his Bible, applied what he'd read to his life and considered his ways, turning it all into communion. Let's try to put into practice this lifestyle priority of getting the Lord in close focus in our lives of service.

BONUS CHAPTER THREE: ONE THING I DESIRE

Single-mindedness is a quality possessed by most, if not all, great performers. If they weren't single-minded, they would never have put in all the hours of preparation, training and rehearsal. Success isn't usually achieved lightly or easily. Paavo Nurmi, the Finnish runner, was brought up in grinding poverty a hundred miles east of Helsinki. His father, a carpenter, died when Paavo was a boy of 12. Young Paavo had to leave school and run errands to support his mother and the rest of the family. He grew up a very gum and gloomy youngster. His only affordable recreation was to practise sprinting by running alongside the railway track in the black pine forest and compete with the mail train as it laboured up the slope.

These runs day after day developed in him a tremendous stamina that would also serve him well as a long-distance runner. Running became his total focus and the obsession of his me. It's been said of him that there's never been such a runner. He won a total of twelve gold and silver Olympic medals. Over ten seasons he set the World Record in every distance he ran. It was with single-minded determination that Nurmi became one of the all-time Olympic greats.

David, king of Israel, is a Bible character with a single-minded focus. Perhaps to many, he's most famous for being the 'competitor' who defeated the giant Goliath in single-handed combat. Later, as king of all Israel, his great successes in the battlefield paved the way for his son Solomon's reign of peace and prosperity. Yet David's heart wasn't set on winning just so that he might enjoy the reputation of being a great warrior. His mind wasn't focused on indulging himself with the spoils of victory. He wasn't someone like Alexander the Great of whom it's said he wept when he thought there was nothing left for him to conquer. David might have been a man of war - and he certainly was - but it was his passion for God that made him tick. That was the real focus and nowhere does that come across more dearly than in Psalm 27. Here are David's own words:

> "The LORD is my light and my salvation; Whom shall I fear? The LORD is the strength of my life; Of whom shall I be afraid? ... Though an army may encamp against me, my heart shall not fear; though war may rise against me, in this I will be confident. One thing I have desired of the LORD, that will I seek: that I may dwell in the house of the LORD all the days of my life, to behold the beauty of the LORD, and to inquire in His temple. For in the time of trouble He shall hide me in His pavilion; in the secret place of His tabernacle He shall hide me; He shall set me high upon a rock. And now my head shall be lifted up above my enemies all around me; therefore I will offer sacrifices of joy ... I will sing, yes, I will sing praises to the LORD" (Psalm 27:1-6).

These are obviously the words of a battle-seasoned veteran. Yet the first thing David acknowledges is the source of his confidence in battle. God was his strength, he said. Just as he had experienced no fear of Goliath, neither had he any fear of opposing armies. He still remained absolutely confident that God was his salvation in every war and military campaign he went into. Then, he really opens his heart when he says, "One thing I have desired of the LORD, that will I seek: That I may dwell in the house of the LORD all the days of my life, to behold the beauty of the LORD, and to inquire in His temple."

Here's the focus, the singe-minded purpose, the driving force of David's life. It was his one great longing. David didn't want to win battles in order to get a bigger castle for himself or a most luxurious life in a more splendid palace. God Himself was the longing of his life. It seems that his role as king was one that he'd willingly have swopped for the life of a priest. The temple, not the palace or castle, was his focus. When surrounded by the threat of attack, he doesn't say: "One thing have I desired, that I may have a stronger army! No, he says, "that I may dwell in the house of the Lord." It was around the courts of God's house that the priests had their lodgings. Did David mean to say he'd have taken his lodging among them? Or, did he mean that he wished he was able - in an undistracted way, without the interruption of war - to constantly attend on the public service of God, with other faithful Israelites? David also said: "I have prepared with all my might: ... I have set my affection on the house of my God, I have given to the house of my God ... my own special treasure of god and silver" (1 Chronicles 29:1-3).

You'll have noticed again that same total focus of David. His all-consuming desire to dwell in the house of the Lord expresses itself again here, as David pledges first his might, then his affection and finally his own special treasure towards the new Temple his son, Solomon, was to build for God at Jerusalem. This was no religious mania. This was the purest spirituality. You can see that from the time when, towards the close of his life, David dedicated his wealth to the magnificent temple structure his son Solomon was to build as a house for God at Jerusalem:

> "David assembled at Jerusalem all the leaders of Israel ... and said, 'Hear me, I had it in my heart to build a house of rest for the ark of the covenant of the LORD, and for the footstool of our God, and had made preparations to build it But God said to me, 'You shall not build a house for My name because you have been a man of war and have shed blood.' ... Now He said to me, 'It is your son

Solomon who shall build My house."' (1 Chronicles 28:1-6)

"Then David gave his son Solomon the plans for the portico of the temple, its buildings, its storerooms, its upper parts, its inner rooms and the place of atonement. He gave him the plans of all that the Spirit had put in his mind for the courts of the temple of the Lord and all the surrounding rooms, for the treasuries of the temple of God and for the treasuries for the dedicated things" (1 Chronicles 28:11-12).

"Furthermore King David said to all the assembly: 'My son Solomon, whom alone God has chosen, is young and inexperienced; and the work is great, because the temple is not for man but for the LORD God'" (1 Chronicles 28:1).

What can we learn from that and apply in our own lives? Is the term 'house of God', which meant so much to David, something we can just use to describe any physical building today that's used as a place of worship? Sometimes we hear it used that way, but do you remember what Stephen, the first Christian martyr, said? He referred back to David, "who found favor before God and asked to find a dwelling for the God of Jacob. But Solomon built Him a house. However, the Most High does not dwell in temples made with hands" (Acts 7:45-48).

The apostle Paul gives us a positive answer later in the Bible to the question, "What was God's house or temple in New Testament times?" In his first letter to the Corinthians, he addresses himself "To the church of God which is at Corinth ... with all who in every place call on the name of Jesus Christ our Lord" (1 Corinthians 1:1-2) and he asks them, "Do you not know that you are ... temple of God and that the Spirit of God dwells in you?" (1 Corinthians 3:16). There's no article in the Greek, so evidently they were 'temple of God' in character.

It wasn't that he was confining this to those faithful disciples in the Church of God at Corinth, but he was extending it to all who were in Bible-based togetherness with them according to Gods pattern of service; so when he comes to chapter 11, he mentions all the churches of God (1 Corinthians 11:16). So, we're left in no doubt that the New Testament writers like Paul had a similar focus to David. It was on the house of God in their day: a focus on a unity among Christians who, being built up together, were following the New Testament pattern of service. Such Christian disciples form God's house on earth. So, where's our focus today? Is our affection set on God's present spiritual house? Do we seek first God's kingdom and his righteous-ness with all our might, or are we taken up with the things of the here and now? Is our treasure laid up on earth or in heaven?

BONUS CHAPTER FOUR: ONE THING I DO

Have you ever wondered about the kind of drive that takes someone where no human has ever been before? In 1953, Sir Edmund Hillary and Tenzing Norgay were the first two men to successfully climb Mount Everest. During an interview in 1996, in answer to a question, Hillary said that 'strong motivation is the most important factor in getting you to the top.' His statement shows us the focus of the mountaineer. No less impressive is the sense of focus that breathes through the apostle Paul's statement given in his Bible letter to friends in Philippi. In the third chapter, Paul says,

> "I ... count all things loss for the excellence of the knowledge of Christ Jesus my Lord, for whom I have suffered the loss of all things, and count them as rubbish, that I may gain Christ and be found in Him, not having my own righteousness, which is from the saw, but that which is through faith in Christ, the righteousness which is from God by faith; that I may know Him and the power of His resurrection, and the fellowship of His sufferings, being conformed to His death, if, by any means, I may attain to the resurrection from the dead.
>
> Not that I have already attained, or am already perfected; but I press on, that I may say hold of that for which Christ Jesus has also laid hold of me. Brethren, I do not count myself to have appre-hended; but one thing I do, forgetting those things which are behind and

reaching forward to those things which are ahead, I press toward the goal for the prize of the upward call of God in Christ Jesus" (Philippians 3:8-14).

Now, perhaps, you see why Paul's statement brought to mind the idea of an uphill climb which demands focused effort. When Paul writes here of gaining Christ he's not thinking about gaining the Saviour and salvation. Not at all! That issue was settled for him long before this. But the apostle Paul was always keen to advance in Christ-like graces. Is that not our own longing: to be more like our Saviour, Jesus Christ? The version quoted from went on to express the desire of Paul to be 'found in him' (Christ). Perhaps it's not immediately clear what that means. A more expanded translation that's sometimes given is: "to be found in Christ by observation" - others observing us to be in Christ. As believers, when we put our faith in God's Son, Jesus, God takes us and places us 'in Christ'. A life of witness should follow, in which we should try to make visible to others around us the fact that we are 'in Christ'. Or to put it another way, we make it visible by our lifestyle that we belong to Jesus.

Maybe you join with me in wishing that others were able to see more of a resemblance between us and our lovely Saviour. Thinking about the Lord Jesus, the hymn writer has written of:

"Those lovely traits

Which in all his earthy days

So beautiful we see."

When we hear those words sung, surely we bow our heads and say, "I'm not there yet, not by a long way." But we can take heart, because Paul goes on in verse 12 of the third chapter of his letter to the Philippians to confess that he's not arrived there either! What he does say is "one thing I do, forgetting those things which are behind and reaching forward to those things which are ahead, I press toward the goal for the prize of the upward call of God in Christ Jesus." Here Paul lays bare his heart, and shares with us the supreme focus of his life. He didn't have 101 things on a 'to do' list; just one! Paul's life was all about doing just 'one thing'. That was pressing on towards the goal of Christ likeness. He knew that God had placed his sovereign grip on his life so that he might reveal his Son in him.

That's what he has in mind when he says: "I press on, that I may lay hold of that for which Christ Jesus has also laid hold of me." He'd once been a misguided fanatic, opposing the will of God through his ignorance, and going in totally the wrong direction. But God had turned him round. God had laid hold of him for a purpose, and Paul was now trying to lay hold of God for the realization of that very same purpose: that other people might come to see the life of Jesus in the life of his follower Paul.

The life of every Christian should be a life moving forward and upward to the goal of Christ-likeness. A year or so ago, I was with a group of young people who had come away for a weekend retreat to study the Bible. On the Saturday afternoon, some recreation time was planned into the programme. We spent it slogging up and down the mountains of Mourne in Northern Ireland. The experience brought to mind Amy Carmichael's poetry:

> "Make us Thy mountaineers
>
> We would not linger on the lower slopes
>
> Fill us afresh with hope, O God of hope
>
> That undefeated we may climb the hill
>
> As seeing him who is invisible.

Let us die climbing.

When this little while lies far behind us

And the last detail is all alight,

And in that light we see

Our Leader and our Lord,

What will it be?"

I think I recall that those words 'let us die climbing' were designed to recall a tragedy on a mountain when some climbers became separated from their party by atrocious conditions. Before they disappeared from view, they were last seen heading to the top. "Let us die climbing' is our prayer. May it be that the last view the world gets of us is of those last seen heading to the top; heading in the upward direction of Christ-likeness. Surely, we don't want to linger on the lower slopes of spiritual mediocrity, but, if we do one thing, let it be pressing on, ever upward, in the upward call of God to the summit of Christ-likeness. In the light of glory, what a tragedy it would be if we'd lingered too long on the lower slopes of mediocre Christian living!

Did you love *Christ-centred Faith*? Then you should read *Daniel Decoded: Deciphering Bible Prophecy* by Brian Johnston!

The Old Testament book of Daniel is perhaps the most half-read in all the Bible! The first half is full of well-loved Sunday School stories and the second half contains complex prophecies about the end times. Brian Johnston explores both halves in this engaging study, which will inspire and inform in equal measure!

CHAPTER ONE: MIGRANTS, AN ALIEN CULTURE AND A HAM SANDWICH

CHAPTER TWO: GOD'S MAN COMES THROUGH

CHAPTER THREE: THE WORLD'S HOTTEST FIRE

CHAPTER FOUR: BECOMING BESTIAL

CHAPTER FIVE: LET THE CRITICS EAT THEIR WORDS

CHAPTER SIX: FACED WITH INJUSTICE

CHAPTER SEVEN: THE RISE AND FALL OF WORLD EMPIRES

CHAPTER EIGHT: THE BRILLIANT MADMAN WHO HATED ISRAEL

CHAPTER NINE: DANIEL'S SEVENTY 'SEVENS'

CHAPTER TEN: SPIRITUAL WARFARE

CHAPTER ELEVEN: THE BIBLE'S MOST DETAILED PROPHETIC CHAPTER

CHAPTER TWELVE: THE END

Also by Brian Johnston

Healthy Churches - God's Bible Blueprint For Growth
Hope for Humanity: God's Fix for a Broken World
First Corinthians: Nothing But Christ Crucified
Bible Answers to Listeners' Questions
Living in God's House: His Design in Action
Christianity 101: Seven Bible Basics
Nights of Old: Bible Stories of God at Work
Daniel Decoded: Deciphering Bible Prophecy
A Test of Commitment: 15 Challenges to Stimulate Your
Devotion to Christ
John's Epistles - Certainty in the Face of Change
If Atheism Is True...
Brian Johnston Box Set 1
8 Amazing Privileges of God's People: A Bible Study of Romans
9:4-5
Learning from Bible Grandparents
Increasing Your Christian Footprint
Christ-centred Faith

About the Author

Born and educated in Scotland, Brian worked as a government scientist until God called him into full-time Christian ministry on behalf of the Churches of God (www.churchesofgod.info). His voice has been heard on Search For Truth radio broadcasts for over 30 years during which time he has been an itinerant Bible teacher throughout the UK and Canada. His evangelical and missionary work outside the UK is primarily in Belgium and The Philippines. He is married to Rosemary, with a son and daughter.

About the Publisher

Hayes Press (www.hayespress.org) is a registered charity in the United Kingdom, whose primary mission is to disseminate the Word of God, mainly through literature. It is one of the largest distributors of gospel tracts and leaflets in the United Kingdom, with over 100 titles and hundreds of thousands despatched annually.

Hayes Press also publishes Plus Eagles Wings, a fun and educational Bible magazine for children, six times a year and Golden Bells, a popular daily Bible reading calendar in wall or desk formats.

Also available are over 100 Bibles in many different versions, shapes and sizes, Christmas cards, Christian jewellery, Eikos Bible Art, Bible text posters and much more!

Printed in Great Britain
by Amazon

37886044R00038